Presented to

_____

By

_____

On

_____

Show & Tell
Bible Stories

50 Stories, Familiar Objects, Fun Rhymes

By Jennifer Holder
Illustrated by Becky Radtke

Standard®
PUBLISHING

Cincinnati, Ohio

Published by Standard Publishing, Cincinnati, Ohio
www.standardpub.com

Copyright © 2010 by Standard Publishing

Printed in: China
Project editors: Elaina Meyers and Christina C. Wallace
Cover and interior illustration: Becky Radtke
Cover and interior design: Sandra S. Wimmer

ISBN 978-0-7847-2129-2

Scripture taken from the Holy Bible, *New Living Translation*, copyright © 1996, 2004. Used by permission of Tyndale House Publishers, Inc., Wheaton, Illinois 60189. All rights reserved.

Library of Congress Cataloging-in-Publication Data

Holder, Jennifer, 1976-
  Show & tell Bible stories : 50 stories, familiar objects, fun rhymes / by Jennifer Holder.
      p. cm.
  ISBN 978-0-7847-2129-2 (casebound)
  1. Bible stories, English. I. Title. II. Title: Show and tell Bible stories.
  BS551.3.H64 2010
  220.9'505--dc22
                                    2010002158

15 14 13 12 11 10   1 2 3 4 5 6 7 8 9

From Jen

For my delightful daughter Beatrice.

From Becky

To my Mom. I have many fond memories of you reading us Bible stories.

Thank you for teaching me about God and living a life that so clearly reflects his love.

OLD TESTAMENT

NEW TESTAMENT

God Made Everything

In the beginning God created the heavens and the earth.
Genesis 1:1

When you make a craft project you use paper and glue
and scissors. You proudly show your work to your teacher
or your mom. God does not need paper, glue, or scissors to
make things. He made the whole world and everything in
it. He was pleased with the work he did.

God said, "Let there be light." And there was light. In the very beginning of everything—the beginning of time and the whole universe—God spoke. His words made things happen.

God made the day and night. Then God made the land and the oceans and the sky above them. He made plants and trees begin to grow. He made the sun and the moon and all the stars. God made all kinds of animals. God did not use paper or glue to form his creation. He created everything out of nothing.

In six days God made the whole world and everything in it. He made it from nothing as only God could. God saw all he created and said, "It is good."

- What is your favorite thing to make? Do you use crayons and paper or glue? What did God use to make the world?
- What are some of the good things God made?

Show & Tell

Now it's your child's turn. Say the rhyme together and help him show and tell that

- God made the whole world in six days.
- God's creation is good.

Show what you made with your own hands.

Tell how God made the sky, sea, and land.

There was empty darkness in the beginning

until God spoke the words that set the world spinning.

Look Who God Made

So God created human beings in his own image.
Genesis 1:27

When you look in your mirror, who do you see? It's you, of course! Take a peek in the mirror to see the face of someone God made in a very special way. God made you in his own image.

After God made the world and all the plants and animals in the world, he still wanted one more creation to add to his masterpiece. He said, "Let us make people in our own image." So God made the first man, Adam. God's creation was "good." After God made people, he said it was "very good."

God made people with mouths and noses on our faces and hair on top of our heads. And God made people with the ability to think thoughts and feel feelings. God gave people eyes and ears. And God gave people hearts so we could love and be loved back. Being made in God's image is a very special thing.

Eyes, ears, mouth, and nose—that's the face the mirror shows. When you look in the mirror, the person you see is made in God's image specially.

- Look in the mirror. What color are your eyes? What color is your hair?
- Use your finger to trace a heart shape on the mirror. You were made to love God and be loved by him.

Show & Tell

Now it's your child's turn. Say the rhyme together and help her show and tell that

- God created people in his own image.
- God created and loves your child.

Show your mirror a face that shines!

Tell how God made his greatest designs.

When he made the good world and all the rest,

God said the people he made were the best.

Adam's Friends

It is not good for the man to be alone. *Genesis 2:18*

Find your favorite, most cuddly teddy bear and give him a big hug. He is a kind of friend who cheers you up when you don't feel well and keeps you company when you're alone. God did not want Adam to be alone. Do you know who God gave to be Adam's friends?

Adam lived in a beautiful garden filled with all the good things God made. He ate tasty fruit from the trees and drank delicious water from the flowing rivers. This wonderful place was called Eden. God put Adam in charge of taking care of Eden.

Then God saw that Adam needed a friend to help him in the garden. God said, "It is not good for the man to be alone." Who could be a good friend for Adam?

God brought the animals he had made to Adam. Maybe one of the birds or cats or lizards would be a good friend for Adam. Adam gave each animal a name, but he didn't find just the right animal friend. So God made a woman named Eve. Eve was the best friend for Adam. They worked together to take care of the animals in the garden.

He met all the animals, but in the end, Eve was the best choice to be Adam's friend.

- What garden was Adam put in charge of?
- What animals do you like?

Show & Tell

Now it's your child's turn. Say the rhyme together and help him show and tell that

- God gives us friends so we won't be alone.
- Adam and Eve took care of the animals in the Garden of Eden.

Show the bear who's always with you.

Tell of the animals Adam knew.

God saw how Adam was in need of a friend,

so he sent the animals for Adam to tend.

Floating Along

As the waters rose higher . . . the boat floated safely
on the surface. *Genesis 7:18*

Think about your bath where you soak and splash. The tub
fills with water and your rubber duck floats and bobs on
the waves you make. The Bible tells of a time when God
filled the whole earth with water. Do you know who floated
and bobbed on the waves of the great flood?

The people in the world had become very bad. God decided to send a flood that would cover the whole earth with water. A flood would wash the world clean.

There was one man who loved God and did right. His name was Noah. God did not want Noah to be washed away in the flood so he told Noah to build an ark. An ark is a kind of boat where Noah and his family could float safely on the water. Guess who else was going to live on the ark. Two of every kind of animal!

Noah made the ark exactly as God told him. God sent the animals to Noah, two by two. They entered the ark and God shut the door. Then the rains came pouring down and the rivers and streams overflowed. The whole earth was covered with water, but God kept Noah, his family, and all the animals safe inside the ark.

God told Noah to build a boat so when the flood came they could stay afloat.

- Who kept Noah and the animals safe from the flood?
- Pretend to be Noah hammering and sawing as he built the ark.

Show & Tell

Now it's your child's turn. Say the rhyme together and help her show and tell that
- a great flood covered the whole earth.
- God saved Noah, his family, and the animals.

Show your ducky and give him a squeeze.
Tell of the ark on the waves of the seas.

On a flood of water that washed the world new,

God saved Noah and the animals too.

The Bird Brought a Leaf

God remembered Noah and all the wild animals and the livestock with him in the boat. *Genesis 8:1*

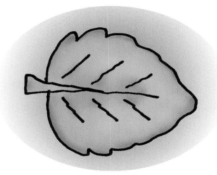

Red and brown leaves on the ground show that trees are getting ready for winter. A new leaf budding on a tree is a sign that the tree is waking up for spring. A leaf was a sign to Noah too. The leaf meant the flood would be over soon.

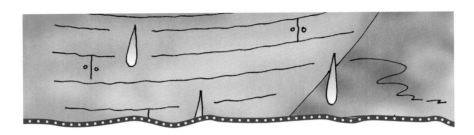

The whole earth was covered with a great flood. Noah and his family, along with two of every kind of animal, were in the ark, riding on the waves.

But God remembered Noah and the ark. He sent a wind to blow across the waters and dry up the flood. Slowly, the water drained away.

Noah sent out a dove from the ark. It was a test to see if the bird could find dry land. The dove returned to Noah, carrying a leaf in her beak. The leaf was a sign that the flood would be over soon.

At last Noah and the animals came out of the ark and stood on dry ground. God promised he would never again flood the whole earth. He put a rainbow in the sky as a reminder of his promise.

The dove brought a leaf to Noah's hand. The leaf was a sign they would soon see dry land.

- Who caused the flood waters to drain away?
- What did the dove bring to Noah as a sign that the flood was almost gone?

Show & Tell

Now it's your child's turn. Say the rhyme together and help him show and tell that

- God drained away the waters of the great flood.
- God promised never to flood the whole earth again.

Show the leaf picked just for you.

Tell of the leaf Noah saw as a clue.

At long last the waters were draining down.

Soon Noah's ark rested on dry ground.

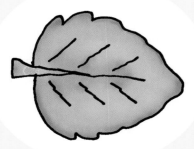

Tower of Bricks

We can make our plans, but the Lord determines our steps. *Proverbs 16:9*

It's fun to stack your bricks up tall. Then knock them down and watch them fall. The people of Babel had bricks too. God did not like what they planned to build with their bricks.

The men of Babel said to each other, "Let's build a great city. All the people will live in our city instead of spreading out across the land." So they made bricks to form the city's walls and streets and houses.

Next they said, "Let's build a great tower. All the people will admire us because our tower reaches to the sky." So they built more. They piled up the bricks, one on top of the other, and the tower grew tall.

But God did not like these plans. He wanted the people to spread out over the land. He wanted the people to be humble instead of seeking glory for building a tall tower. God went down to Babel and confused the people. Their language became mixed up. They could not understand each other and so they stopped building. The people left the city and the tower and they scattered all over the world.

They built with bricks to gain some fame, but stopped when their language wasn't the same.

- What did the people of Babel plan to build?
- See how high you can make a tower of blocks before it falls down.

Show & Tell

Now it's your child's turn. Say the rhyme together and help her show and tell that

- God did not like the people's plans for a great city and tower.
- God caused the people of Babel to speak different languages.

Show your blocks and stack them up high.

Tell how some bricks towered into the sky.

The men of Babel tried to build to the top,

but their mixed-up language brought the work to

a stop.

God's Shining Promise

I will certainly bless you. I will multiply your descendants beyond number, like the stars in the sky. *Genesis 22:17*

Every night the light in your room glows softly while you sleep. Every night the stars glowing in the sky remind us of the promises God keeps.

The stars shone in the sky over Abraham's hometown, but Abraham was not there. God told Abraham, "Leave your father's home and come to a new land I am giving you." Abraham trusted God, so he packed up his household and moved far away.

The stars shone in the sky over the land of Canaan, where Abraham made his new home. God told Abraham, "This land will belong to you and your children." Abraham built an altar and worshiped God.

The stars shone in the sky night after night over Abraham's tent. God told Abraham, "Look up to the sky and count the stars, if you can. That's how many descendants you will have. I make you into a great nation. I will bless the whole world through your children."

Abraham believed God's promise.

- Who told Abraham to count the stars?
- What was God's promise to Abraham?

Show & Tell

Now it's your child's turn. Say the rhyme together and help him show and tell that

- the many stars showed God's promise that Abraham would have many children.
- Abraham trusted God's promise.

Show the light twinkling in your room's darkness.
Tell of the stars God showed as a promise.

God promised to give to Abraham's line

more children than there are stars in the sky.

Finally a Family

Abraham was 100 years old when Isaac was born.
Genesis 21:5

It is good to be part of a family. There is a special excitement when God sends a new baby to a family. Imagine how much more excitement there was when a new baby came to a father who was more than 100 years old!

God had promised to make Abraham a father. Abraham believed God's promise, but it was so hard waiting! As more and more years passed, Abraham and Sarah began to wonder how they could ever have a baby in their family.

Finally, when Abraham and Sarah were both very old, God came to Abraham's home. "The time is right for you and Sarah to have a son," God said. When Sarah heard the wonderful news, she couldn't help laughing. "I am 90 years old and Abraham is nearly 100. How can we have a baby now?" she asked.

God said, "Nothing is too hard for me to do!" Sure enough, just as God promised, Sarah and Abraham soon had a baby boy. They named him Isaac, which means "laughter." And they were a very happy family.

- Who promised to give Abraham and Sarah a son?
- What did Abraham and Sarah name their baby?

Show & Tell

Now it's your child's turn. Say the rhyme together and help her show and tell that

- Isaac was born when Abraham and Sarah were very old.
- God kept his promise to give Abraham a son.

Show the family whose love you know.

Tell of a family from a time long ago.

Abraham and Sarah, though they were old,

were delighted to have a son to hold.

Joseph's Beautiful Coat

Jacob had a special gift made for Joseph—
a beautiful robe. *Genesis 37:3*

It's special to wear beautiful clothes, but the best thing
about a coat is that it keeps you warm when it's cold
outside. The best thing about Joseph's coat was that it was
a gift from his father who loved him. The worst thing was
that it made his brothers jealous.

Jacob had many sons, but he loved one son more than the others. For this son, Joseph, Jacob made a very special, colorful coat. Joseph's brothers were jealous of the beautiful coat and the special treatment Joseph got from their father. They decided to get rid of him. Joseph was sold as a slave and taken to Egypt.

Even though he was a slave, Joseph continued to honor God and do right. God caused Joseph to become a governor who saved the whole country from a terrible famine. God had made the bad thing Joseph's brothers did into a good thing that saved many people from starvation.

Joseph forgave his brothers for what they had done. He and the father who loved him so much were able to be together again.

Joseph's brothers were up to no good, but God made it right as only he could.

- Who gave Joseph a beautiful coat?
- What's the best thing about your coat?

Show & Tell

Now it's your child's turn. Say the rhyme together and help him show and tell that

- Joseph's brothers were jealous of his coat.
- God made something good happen from a bad thing.

Show the coat that's been given to you.
Tell of a coat with red, green, orange, and blue.

Joseph's colorful coat got him in a tight spot,

but God made good come out of the awful plot.

Tucked Into a Basket

The princess named him Moses, for she explained,
"I lifted him out of the water." *Exodus 2:10*

What treasures does your basket hold? The Egyptian
princess was surprised by what she found in a basket one
day. Do you know what it was?

The mother prayed as she wove the stalks together to form a strong basket. "God, please keep my baby safe and hidden from Pharaoh." When the basket was finished, she tucked her son into it and placed it among the reeds on the bank of the Nile River.

The baby's sister stayed close by to see what would happen. Soon a princess came to the river to take a bath. *"Waah! Waah!"* was the crying sound the princess heard. It was coming from the basket!

The princess pulled the basket from the water and hugged the baby hidden inside. "I will adopt this child. He will live with me in the palace as my son. I will name him Moses."

Moses' sister left the basket behind. She ran to tell their mother what had happened. As the river carried the basket-bed, God answered the prayers Moses' mother had said.

- Why did the mother make a basket for her baby?
- Who was the baby the princess found in a basket?

Show & Tell

Now it's your child's turn. Say the rhyme together and help her show and tell that

- baby Moses was hidden in a basket.
- God safely guided Moses' basket to the princess.

Show your basket woven from straw.

Tell of the princess and the baby she saw.

From a basket in the river, Moses' cries filled the air

until God floated him to the princess's care.

48

Walking Across the Sea

With the power of his mighty hand, the Lord brought us out of Egypt. *Exodus 13:14*

What places do you go in your car? To school? To visit a friend? Have you ever taken an airplane to visit someplace far, far away? In the time of Moses, God's people made a very long journey. But they did not have a car to ride in or a plane to fly in.

God's people were ready to go. They gathered their belongings quickly. They put on their travelling sandals and found their walking sticks. Soon they began walking away from the land of Egypt.

But Pharaoh wanted Israel to stay and keep working as his slaves. He decided to send an army of 600 chariots to chase after God's people. How could they outrun horses and chariots? The people came to the shore of the Red Sea. They turned and watched as Pharaoh's army came closer and closer.

Moses told the people, "Don't be afraid. God will rescue you today." Then God sent a great wind over the Red Sea. He opened up a path of dry land right through the middle of the sea. The people crossed on dry land. But when Pharaoh's chariots reached the sea, God caused the water to crash back down over the path. All of Pharaoh's army was swept away.

God's mighty hand saved his people that day. He parted the sea and his people got away.

- Who made a journey out of Egypt?
- Who parted the waters of the Red Sea?

Show & Tell

Now it's your child's turn. Say the rhyme together and help him show and tell that

- God brought his people out of Egypt.
- God's people crossed the Red Sea on dry land.

Show how you travel: by plane, train, or car.

Tell of how Israel journeyed so far.

God's people left Egypt; they were no longer slaves.

They traveled on foot to the new land God gave.

Love God with Your Heart

Love the Lord your God with all your heart, all your soul, and all your strength. *Deuteronomy 6:5*

Trace the shape of a heart on your chest. That is a symbol of love. Someone who loves you might give you a valentine shaped like a heart. Following what God says is like giving him a valentine every day.

God set up a law for his people to follow. God loves us and made rules that are very good for us. God wrote his ten rules, or commandments, on stone tablets. Moses called the whole nation of Israel together and read the ten rules to the people:

1. Only worship God.
2. Don't make or bow down to an idol.
3. Honor God's name.
4. Remember God's day of rest.
5. Honor your father and mother.
6. Don't murder.
7. Husbands and wives should be faithful to each other.
8. Don't steal.
9. Tell the truth.
10. Don't be jealous of what others have.

Moses reminded God's people of all the good and mighty things God had done for them. Then he said, "We should love God with everything we have—our heart, soul, and strength." We can love God by obeying the commands he gave.

- How many rules, or commandments, did God give?
- How can we love God?

Show & Tell

Now it's your child's turn. Say the rhyme together and help her show and tell that
- God gave ten commandments.
- we love God by obeying his commands.

Show the heart, love's symbol in red.
Tell, "Heart, soul, and strength," the words
       Moses said.
We show God our love when we obey
his ten commandments every day.

55

The Scarlet Cord

I know the Lord has given you this land. Joshua 2:9

Tie a red ribbon around a box to make a pretty birthday present. Or tie a red string around your finger to help you remember something important. The red cord tied in Rahab's window was a special sign in the battle of Jericho.

Two spies sneaked into the city of Jericho. A battle was coming and the two had been sent to scout the city. Quietly they knocked on the door of Rahab's house.

Everyone inside the city walls had heard about God's power and how he fought for his people. Rahab had heard this too. She told the spies, "I believe your God will win the coming battle. I will help you tonight. When the fighting comes, I will trust you and your God to save me."

The officials from the city soon came looking for the two spies. Rahab hid the men then she helped them escape. The spies made an agreement with Rahab. "Tie a red cord in your window as a sign to us. Then you will be safe."

Soon God's people marched around the walls of Jericho. God destroyed the city, but Rahab and all her family were safe. The sign in her window was a scarlet cord because Rahab believed in the power of the Lord.

- How did Rahab help the spies?
- What did Rahab tie in her window?

58

Show & Tell

Now it's your child's turn. Say the rhyme together and help him show and tell that
- Rahab believed in God's power.
- Jericho was destroyed but Rahab was saved.

Show your ribbon and tie it in a bow.

Tell of the cord in Rahab's window.

Rahab feared the Lord, so she helped the spies hide.

The cord was a sign that Rahab chose God's side.

Stacked Up Stones

These stones will stand as a memorial among the people of Israel forever. *Joshua 4:7*

Where did you find the stone that you are holding? Maybe at a park or in your own backyard? The stones that God's people collected came from the bottom of the Jordan River!

God's people stood at the banks of the Jordan River watching the water flow swiftly by. It was time for them to enter the new land God was giving them but the river was blocking their way. How would they get across?

God said to his people, "Step into the river. I will make the water stop flowing." The people took a few steps into the river. Soon the water stopped and the riverbed became completely dry.

God said, "Take twelve stones from the middle of the river. Carry them out and pile them up in your camp." So twelve men picked up twelve stones from the middle of the river. They carried them to the camp. After this was done, and after all of God's people had crossed on dry ground, God sent the river waters rushing back in.

The people made the stones into a memorial. Joshua, the leader of God's people, said, "This stack of stones helps us remember and know how God made the river stop its flow."

- Who caused the Jordan River to dry up?

- What did God's people take from the middle of the river?

Show & Tell

Now it's your child's turn. Say the rhyme together and help her show and tell that

- God's people crossed the Jordan River on dry ground.
- the people stacked up twelve stones as a reminder of what God did.

Show the stone you were able to find.

Tell of the stones Israel used as a sign.

They took stones from the Jordan and stacked them up tall

to remind them of what God had done for them all.

Receive God's Good Gifts

Every good and perfect gift is from above. *James 1:17*

What good things does your bag hold for you? Your favorite books? Your toys? A snack? Ruth was a woman who started out with nothing but ended up holding lots of good things—lots of good gifts from God.

Ruth and her mother-in-law, Naomi, trudged along the road. Their bags were nearly empty, because they were poor widows with only a few possessions. Their food sacks were completely empty because they were leaving a place where there was no food.

They traveled together to Bethlehem. There God gave good food to Ruth and Naomi. Ruth worked in the field of a man named Boaz. She walked behind the harvesters picking up the stalks and kernels they left behind.

One night Boaz said to Ruth, "You are an honest woman who has been very faithful to your family. God will reward you." Then he filled her shawl, like a bag, with even more grain for her food.

Boaz and Ruth made an agreement to be married. God's reward to Ruth was a kind husband, Boaz, and a son, Obed.

Ruth started out empty, but became fully blessed. God's plan for Ruth was to give her the best.

- What blessings did God give to Ruth?

- What are some good things God gives you?

Show & Tell

Now it's your child's turn. Say the rhyme together and help him show and tell that

- God gave Ruth good grain to eat.
- God gave Ruth a kind husband and a son.

Show your bag that is roomy inside.

Tell how Ruth trusted God to provide.

Ruth's shawl was empty when her journey began,

but she came away full of good gifts from God's hand.

It Is Good to Sing Praises to God

Praise the Lord! How good to sing praises to our God!
Psalm 147:1

Do you ever wonder if God can hear it when you strum your guitar or tap, tap, tap on your drum? He can! The next time you want to play some music, make a song of praise to God.

Psalm 150 says, "Praise the Lord for his power and great deeds. Praise him with music and dancing. Praise him with the trumpet and harp. Everyone should praise the Lord!" God is so great and good. He is worthy of all the praise we can give him. Our praises make God happy.

The man who wrote Psalm 150 was an expert on praising God—especially with music. His name was David. As a young boy, David played music in the fields as he tended his sheep. Later he played songs in the royal palace to soothe the king of Israel.

All his life, David wrote sacred poems or songs called psalms. He wrote about God's strength and protection. He wrote about God's goodness and wisdom. There came a time when God made David king of the whole nation of Israel. David continued to praise God.

David picked out some notes and soon he was praising God with his pleasing tune.

- What are the special songs that David wrote called?

- What are some great things about God that you can praise him for?

Show & Tell

Now it's your child's turn. Say the rhyme together and help her show and tell that

- God deserves our praise.
- it is good to praise God with music.

Show the instrument where sweet music plays.

Tell about one who praised God all his days.

David praised God with music and song.

We read David's psalms and sing along.

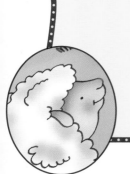

Small Like David, Tall Like Goliath

This is the Lord's battle. *1 Samuel 17:47*

Standing up on your stepstool makes you bigger and taller.
Now you can reach the bathroom sink or grab a book from
the highest shelf. Goliath stood bigger and taller too, but
not because of a stool.

Goliath was so big and tall that no one in all of Israel would face him in a fight. They were too terrified. Every day Goliath came to the battlefield carrying a heavy sword. Shaking his huge spear and javelin, he taunted God's people.

David was a young boy. He was not a soldier, but a shepherd who took care of his father's sheep. When David heard Goliath shouting insults, he decided to take action.

"Don't be ridiculous!" said the king. "A boy cannot win against a giant." David told the king, "Goliath stands against God and his people. The Lord will help me defeat this enemy."

The tall giant and the small boy came face to face on the battlefield. As Goliath charged toward him, David reached into his bag. David pulled out his slingshot and one smooth stone. He hurled the stone and the giant Goliath fell down flat!

Goliath was big and David was small, but the battle belonged to God after all.

- Step on your stool and be tall like Goliath. Now be small like David.

- Who did David believe could win the battle against a giant?

Show & Tell

Now it's your child's turn. Say the rhyme together and help him show and tell that

- the giant Goliath was defeated.
- David relied on God and won the battle.

Show the stool that helps you stand tall.
Tell of the giant and the boy so small.

Goliath came to battle with a sword and a spear,

but David called on God so he had no fear.

Jonathan and David Share Friendship

Jonathan said to David, ". . . We have sworn loyalty to each other in the Lord's name." *1 Samuel 20:42*

A ball is a fun thing to have—especially when you share it with a friend. A friend is someone who shares good times with you and also helps you when you are in trouble. The Bible tells about someone who was a very good friend to David.

77

David had a friend named Jonathan. Jonathan was the son of Saul, the king. Like David, Jonathan was a warrior. He led the king's army in battles. Like David, Jonathan trusted the Lord to defeat Israel's enemies.

Jonathan's father, King Saul, was very jealous of Jonathan's and David's fighting skill. Saul especially hated David. He made a plan to kill David. But Jonathan was loyal to his friend. He found out about his father's evil plot. Jonathan told David, "Run away and hide! You are in danger from my father, Saul!"

Jonathan and David made an agreement that they and all their children would be faithful friends. Many years later, after David became king, he still showed kindness to his old friend Jonathan.

Jonathan and David were faithful friends. They were kind and loyal to the end.

- How were David and Jonathan alike?

- Who are your favorite friends?

Show & Tell

Now it's your child's turn. Say the rhyme together and help her show and tell that

- Jonathan and David were good friends to each other.
- when David was in danger, Jonathan was loyal to him.

Show the ball that you bounce to a friend.
Tell of a friend on whom David could depend.

In a time that was full of fighting and fear,

David was glad his friend Jonathan stayed near.

King Solomon's Dream

I will give you a wise and understanding heart.
1 Kings 3:12

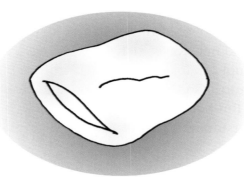

"Sweet dreams!" we say as we snuggle into our pillow each night and get ready for sleep. You probably have never had a dream like the one King Solomon had one night long ago. While Solomon rested on his royal pillow, God himself appeared.

Solomon learned from his father David to love God and obey God's laws. One night, after Solomon worshiped at God's altar, the Lord appeared to him in a dream. God said to Solomon, "What do you want? Ask and I will give it to you."

Solomon did not ask for riches. He did not ask for fame. Solomon did not ask for a long life. Solomon did ask for wisdom. He said, "God, you have made me king over your great people. But I do not know the best way to lead them. Give me understanding so that I can be a good king for your people."

God was very pleased that Solomon had asked this. He made Solomon very wise—the wisest man ever to have lived. God also gave Solomon riches and fame and a long life even though Solomon did not ask for these things.

He rested on his pillow and closed his eyes. While he dreamed, Solomon chose to be wise.

- What did Solomon ask God to give him?
- If God came to your dream tonight, what would you ask for?

Show & Tell

Now it's your child's turn. Say the rhyme together and help him show and tell that

- Solomon asked God for wisdom.
- God gave Solomon wisdom and wealth.

Show the pillow where you lay your head.
Tell of the words King Solomon said.

He asked for wisdom for his rule.

God gave him that and riches too.

Tools for the Temple

I am planning to build a Temple to honor the name of the Lord my God. *1 Kings 5:5*

Bang! Bang! Bang! That's the sound your hammer makes as you create a project with your tools. King Solomon needed a lot of tools. He needed workers and supplies too. What was Solomon building that was so big and important?

*B*ang! *Bang!* The workers' hammers pounded away at the planks of wood. *Chink! Chink!* The stonecutters' chisels shaped the heavy stones. These were the sounds King Solomon heard when he visited the men who were working on God's temple.

Solomon was very wise so he followed God's instructions for how this special place should be built. He hired skilled workers. He ordered the timber from the strongest trees. He chose stones of the finest quality.

The temple was filled with beautiful carvings and decorations. The furniture and dishes and lamps inside the temple were made of gold. Solomon gave the very best for God.

After seven years of work, at last the building was complete. Solomon called all of God's people to come and dedicate the wonderful temple to God. Solomon prayed and the people sang praises to honor God.

The men worked with their tools each day. The finished temple was filled with God's praise.

- What did Solomon build?

- What were some of the things inside the temple?

Show & Tell

Now it's your child's turn. Say the rhyme together and help her show and tell that

- Solomon built a temple to honor God.
- the people prayed and sang praises at God's temple.

Show the tools that you turn, tap, and tilt.

Tell of the temple that Solomon built.

Wood, stone, and gold formed by the hammers' bang

made a place where God's people prayed and sang.

Naaman's Wonderful Wash

Go and wash and be cured! *2 Kings 5:13*

Bubble bath makes it fun to scrub in the tub. But what if someone told you to take a bath seven times in a row?

Naaman was an important man in his country's army. Though he was wealthy and successful, Naaman suffered because he had a skin disease called leprosy. A young servant girl in Naaman's house believed that God had the power to heal her master. She said, "God's prophet Elisha can help you." So Naaman traveled to Israel and asked Elisha for help.

A messenger brought Elisha's instructions to Namman: "Go and wash in the Jordan River seven times."

Naaman did not want to do this. Finally Naaman decided to follow Elisha's instructions anyway. One, two, three times he dipped in the cold river. Four, five, six times he washed. On the seventh time, Naaman was healed! The leprosy was gone and his skin was clean. Naaman believed in God. "From now on, I will only worship the one true God," said Naaman.

Seven splashes in the Jordan cleaned his skin from toe to head. "I will only worship God," was what the healed man said.

- Who told Naaman about God's prophet Elisha?

- How many times did Naaman wash?

Show & Tell

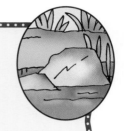

Now it's your child's turn. Say the rhyme together and help him show and tell that
- Naaman washed seven times in the Jordan River.
- God healed Naaman.

Show the bubbles that get you clean in your tub.

Tell of the man who scrubbed, scrubbed, and

    scrubbed!

He washed seven times—not eight, nine, or ten.

In the Jorden River, God made Naaman healthy again!

Beautiful, Brave Esther

He set the royal crown on her head and declared
her queen. *Esther 2:17*

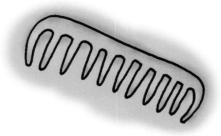

Brush your hair until it shines. Now imagine a shiny crown
sitting there. King Xerxes placed a crown on Esther's lovely
head. The king chose Esther because she was beautiful,
but God helped her to be brave too.

Esther brushed her long hair and decorated it with a jeweled comb. She dressed in a beautiful gown and sprayed a delicious-smelling perfume. After all, she was a queen living in a wonderful palace.

One day, Esther learned of a terrible plot. The king's official wanted to get rid of God's people. The king agreed to do it! No one knew that Esther was one of God's people too.

The rule in the palace was, "Do not come to the king unless he calls you." But Esther could not wait to be called. She must stop the plot against God's people!

Esther prayed to God for help and then bravely stepped into the king's throne room. The king was happy to see Esther. She was not in trouble for breaking the rule after all. The king agreed to save God's people from destruction.

Esther's beauty won the king's good will. Her standing bravely for God's people was better still.

- What brave thing did Esther do?
- Who helped Esther be brave?

Show & Tell

Now it's your child's turn. Say the rhyme together and help her show and tell that

- Esther was a beautiful queen.
- Esther's bravery saved God's people.

Show the comb that tames your curls.

Tell the story of a beautiful girl.

Queen Esther was lovely and also brave.

Because of her actions, God's people were saved.

Daniel and the Lions

May your God, whom you serve so faithfully, rescue you.
Daniel 6:16

A toy lion is fun to hug and cuddle, but a real lion is a fearsome thing! Pretend to growl like a huge lion and show all your sharp teeth. Now pretend to be like the lions in the story of Daniel. What did they do different?

The lions paced the floor of their cave. The licked their sharp teeth and got ready to bite! King Darius and his officials stood with Daniel outside the cave. The king was sad. He did not want to throw Daniel in with the ferocious lions. But Daniel had broken the law—Daniel had prayed to God even though the law said not to—so now he must face the punishment.

The king said, "You are a man who prays and trusts God. I hope your God will save you from these lions." Then he closed the mouth of the cave. Daniel was trapped inside.

The next morning King Darius hurried out to the lions' den. He called, "Daniel, did God save you?"

Daniel answered, "My God sent an angel to shut the lions' mouths. They did not hurt me." King Darius was very happy. He sent a message to all the people in his land. "The God of Daniel will live forever. He rescues and saves his people," wrote the king.

- Who prayed and trusted God?
- Who did God send to shut the lions' mouths?

Show & Tell

Now it's your child's turn. Say the rhyme together and help him show and tell that

- Daniel prayed and trusted God.
- God saved Daniel from the lions.

Show your toy lion with ears, nose, and toes.

Tell of the lions whose mouths God closed.

Daniel prayed to God and God kept him safe

through the night Daniel spent in the lions' dark cave.

The Baby's Name

Name him Jesus, for he will save his people from their sins.
Matthew 1:21

Your parents chose your name because it had a good sound and meaning to them. Now it's written on the special things that belong only to you. The name God gave his Son has a very special meaning. The name Jesus means *God saves.*

A new baby was on the way. What would his name be? This baby was coming to be the Savior and King of all God's people. So God gave him a special name. The baby's name made the world know the special job he would do one day.

An angel announced the baby's name. He said, "Mary, God is going to bless you. You are going to have a son. His name will be Jesus."

The angel told Joseph, the man who would be Mary's husband, the meaning of the baby's special name. The angel said, "His name will be Jesus, because he will save people from their sins."

God and the angels and God's prophets all knew of the important work Jesus would one day do. God's Son would come to save, so Jesus is the name the angel gave. Hooray! God's promised Savior was on his way!

- Who announced the baby's special name?
- What did the angel say Jesus would do?

Show & Tell

Now it's your child's turn. Say the rhyme together and help her show and tell that
- the angel said, "His name will be Jesus."
- Jesus' name means *God saves*.

Show the name your parents gave you.

Tell of the name the angels knew.

The name given to God's Son at his birth

is a clue to what Jesus would do on this earth.

Special Baby, Special Blanket

You will find the baby wrapped snugly in strips of cloth, lying in a manger. Luke 2:12

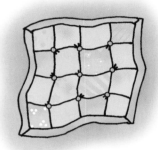

Do you have a special blanket? Pull it close and cuddle up. This blanket keeps you warm while you sleep every night. Another little one also had a blanket to snuggle while he slept. Do you know who it was?

Long ago a special baby was born. He was Jesus, God's Son. He came to save us and to show how much God loves us.

That night, an angel appeared to some shepherds in the fields nearby. "Tonight your Savior has been born in Bethlehem," the angel said. "You will find him wrapped up with cloth and lying in a manger bed."

The shepherds ran to the town to see the new baby king in a blanket. They were so happy to meet Jesus!

A blanket reminds us of what the shepherds saw—baby Jesus bundled up, asleep in the straw.

- What is nice about your blanket? Do you think baby Jesus was comfy in his manger bed?

- Pretend to wrap up baby Jesus in your blanket. How would you lay him in the manger?

Show & Tell

Now it's your child's turn. Say the rhyme together and help him show and tell that

- Jesus came to show God's love for us!
- the shepherds found baby Jesus wrapped in cloths and lying in a manger.

Show your blanket, cozy and warm.

Tell of the night when Jesus was born.

Remember the manger as you snuggle up tight.

God's love came down to Earth that night.

Jesus Grew

Jesus grew in wisdom and in stature and in favor with God. *Luke 2:52*

Do you ever feel like it will take forever before you grow up enough to do the things you want to do? If you look at some old clothes that you used to wear, you can see how far you've come. You're growing up! Jesus was born as a baby but soon he grew into a boy and then into a man.

*J*esus' parents were looking everywhere for their boy. The whole family was traveling home after a visit to the temple. *Where could he have gone?* they wondered. They asked all of Jesus' friends and relatives, "Have you seen our boy?"

Jesus was not really lost. He was in the temple courts, sitting with the teachers, listening and asking them questions. Everyone who heard Jesus was amazed at how much he understood.

Finally Mary and Joseph came back to the temple. They were amazed to find Jesus there. "We have been looking for you!" Joseph told Jesus.

"Didn't you know I had to be in my Father's house?" Jesus replied. Jesus was saying that the temple was God's house and God was his heavenly father. Then Jesus went back home with Mary and Joseph and obeyed them. He continued to grow taller and stronger as well as wiser. Jesus continued to please God.

- What was Jesus doing in the temple courts?
- Who grew taller, stronger, and wiser?

Show & Tell

Now it's your child's turn. Say the rhyme together and help her show and tell that

- Jesus was found in the temple, God's house.
- Jesus grew taller and stronger and wiser.

Show your old clothes now too small for you.

Tell about how Jesus grew bigger too.

As Jesus grew up, he became wise and strong.

He said, "In my Father's house is where I belong."

The Messenger in the Wilderness

I am sending my messenger ahead of you, and he will prepare your way. *Mark 1:2*

Is pizza your favorite food? Maybe ice cream is your favorite treat. Sometimes the food we eat is a clue to where we are. A boy living in India might choose curry as his favorite. A girl living in Japan might pick dried octopus. The Bible tells about a man who ate locusts. Why would anyone do that?

John the Baptist lived in the wilderness. His life was very simple compared to most people. He did not eat rich foods. Instead he ate locusts and wild honey. He did not wear expensive clothes. Instead he wore a cloak made of camel hair and a leather belt.

God sent John the Baptist to tell people to get ready! God's Son, Jesus, was about to begin his work. John said, "God's Son is coming to save us. Get your hearts ready for him." People came to John to be baptized in the Jordan River.

Jesus came to be baptized too. When Jesus came up from the water, God's Spirit came from Heaven like a dove. A voice from Heaven said, "You are my Son. I love you. I am pleased with you."

John the Baptist did the job God had for him. He pointed to Jesus and said, "Look! He is the one who will save us from sin."

- Who did God send to help people get ready for Jesus' coming?
- What did John the Baptist eat?

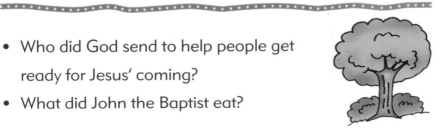

Show & Tell

Now it's your child's turn. Say the rhyme together and help him show and tell that

- John baptized Jesus in the Jordan River.
- John said, "Jesus is God's Son who will save us."

Show the food you like best to eat.
Tell of a locust-and-honey treat.

John lived, dressed, and ate in a simple way

and God gave him a special message to say.

Fishers of People

Jesus called out to them, "Come, follow me." *Mark 1:17*

Crunch, crunch. That is the sound your mouth makes as you eat delicious fish crackers. *Splash, splash* is the sound of a slippery fish caught in the fishermen's nets. "I will make you fishers of men," was the next sound those fishermen heard.

One day, as Jesus was walking along the shore of the sea, he saw two brothers casting fishing nets into the water. Jesus called out to them, "Come, follow me!" Jesus said, "I will show you how to fish for people." The fishermen, Simon and Andrew, immediately left their nets to follow Jesus.

A little father up the shore, Jesus saw James and John. They were also fishermen. Jesus called out, "Come, follow me!" James and John left their boats behind and followed Jesus.

These men, along with several others, became Jesus' close friends. They traveled with Jesus and saw how he showed God's care for people and God's power. They listened to Jesus' teachings about God's wonderful love. They became fishers of people, just as Jesus promised, by telling others about Jesus' love. Fishing for people is what Jesus said to do. Tell others about Jesus so they can follow him too.

- Have you ever gone fishing? What did you catch?
- What did Jesus call out to the fishermen?

Show & Tell

Now it's your child's turn. Say the rhyme together and help her show and tell that

- Jesus said, "Come, follow me!"
- the fishermen left their nets and their boats to follow Jesus.

Show the crackers shaped like fish in the sea.

Tell of the fishermen from Galilee.

"Come, follow me," were the words Jesus said.

So the fishermen followed where Jesus led.

A Very Special Drink

But those who drink the water I give will never be thirsty again. John 4:14

When you're thirsty, a cool drink from your cup tastes so good! In Jesus' day, cool water drawn from a well tasted good to thirsty people.

Jesus sat beside a well after a long, dusty walk. "Please give me a drink," he said to a woman there.

The woman was very surprised that Jesus was speaking to her. "Why are you asking me for a drink?" she asked.

Jesus answered, "If only you knew about a special kind of water I can give you. Then *you* would ask *me* for a drink." Then Jesus began to talk to the woman about living water. Jesus said, "Whoever drinks the water I give will never be thirsty again."

But Jesus' living water does not come from a well. He was talking about a special water for our hearts that only Jesus can give. Jesus' living water brings never-ending life for people who believe in Jesus.

The woman left her water jar and ran back to the village to tell everyone what Jesus had said. Many Samaritans believed in Jesus.

The woman who met Jesus at the well ran back to her home with good news to tell.

Who did Jesus meet at a well in Samaria?

What kind of water did Jesus say he would give?

Show & Tell

Now it's your child's turn. Say the rhyme together and help him show and tell that
- Jesus gives us eternal life.
- the woman at the well believed Jesus.

Show your cup and take a sip.

Tell of water jars that drip, drip, dripped.

The woman at the well found Jesus can give

water that makes us eternally live.

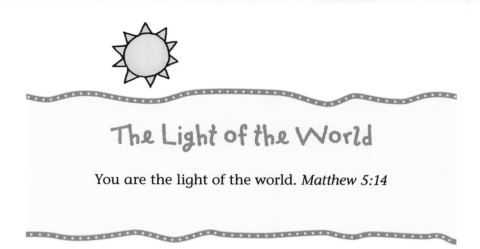

The Light of the World

You are the light of the world. *Matthew 5:14*

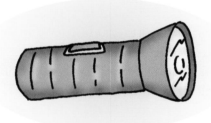

Shine your flashlight down a dark hallway. The light helps you see which way you should go. People who love Jesus are like lights that show other people the way to go.

Jesus traveled across the countryside teaching the people about God's love and his kingdom. Many people followed him. They loved to listen to his lessons.

One day Jesus taught, "You are the light of the world. You are like a lamp lit in a house. Should you hide the bright light you give? No! Give light to everyone in the house."

What did Jesus mean? How can a person be like a light? Jesus was saying we should never hide our love for him. Instead, he wants us to show everyone that we do right things because we love Jesus. Other people can see the good things that happen when we follow and obey God's Word. People will know that God is great and give him praise.

What we do and what we say shows our neighbors God's goodness every day.

- Who said, "You are the light of the world?"
- How can a person be like a light?

Show & Tell

Now it's your child's turn. Say the rhyme together and help her show and tell that
- God's people are the light of the world.
- we should let our lights shine.

Show the beam of your flashlight.

Tell how your life can shine so bright.

Jesus said, "You are the light the world needs.

Others will give God the praise for your deeds."

God's Wonderful Care

If God cares so wonderfully for wildflowers . . .
he will certainly care for you. *Matthew 6:30*

The flower you picked looks very beautiful because of its fresh leaves and colorful petals. Do you know who gave the flower its leaves and petals?

Jesus went up on a mountainside and continued to teach about God. A large crowd came to hear what Jesus had to say.

Jesus pointed to the birds flying from tree to tree. "How do the birds get food?" Jesus asked. "The birds don't plant crops. They don't store up food. They have enough to eat because God feeds them," he taught.

Then he pointed to the flowers growing by the mountain. "Do the flowers spend money to get rich clothes?" Jesus asked. "The flowers don't work or sew clothing. Still they are beautifully dressed with colorful petals. God is the one who takes care of them."

Jesus told the people, "See, God takes care of little things like birds and flowers. But his people—you!—are so much more important than birds or flowers. He loves you so much more! So do not worry. Instead, trust God to give you what you need."

- Who gives the birds enough to eat?
- Who should you trust to give what you need?

Show & Tell

Now it's your child's turn. Say the rhyme together and help him show and tell that

- God takes care of the flowers and birds.
- God takes care of his people.

Show the flower you picked from the earth.

Tell of something with much more worth.

God cares for the flowers and feeds the birds too,

but God cares oh, so much more for you!

How to Talk to God

Never stop praying. *1 Thessalonians 5:17*

When you call a friend on your phone, you share what you are doing and thinking that day. Or you tell them about some help you need. Talking to God is like talking to a friend, except instead of using a phone, you use a prayer.

Every day, while he was on Earth, Jesus talked to God. He found a quiet place to be alone and prayed there.

One day Jesus taught his followers about talking to God. Jesus gave his followers this example:

Dear Father in Heaven, you are holy.

Please be in charge of our lives here and now
and help us do the things you want us to do.

Give us what we need each day.

Forgive us when we do wrong and help us forgive
others too.

Help us to stay away from trouble. Save us from evil.

God loves to hear from us. He wants to know what we think about and what we need. We need to tell him that we love him and are thankful for his good gifts.

Jesus used prayer to talk to God every day. You can talk to God in the same way.

- How often did Jesus talk to God?

- What are some things you want to say to God right now?

Show & Tell

Now it's your child's turn. Say the rhyme together and help her show and tell that

- Jesus talked to God every day.
- God listens to our prayers.

Show the phone that calls friends far and near.
Tell about all the prayers God hears.

When you pray to God, you talk and listen too.

God is a friend who always hears you.

A Meal to Share

And they all ate as much as they wanted. *John 6:11*

At lunch, we get our bellies full with spoonfuls of cheesy macaroni or crispy pieces of chicken. That meal is the fuel you need to keep going strong for the rest of the day. Now try to imagine sharing your mac and cheese meal with more than 5,000 people. How could there possibly be enough food for everyone?

One day a young boy went to hear what Jesus was teaching about God. As the day went on, the boy's tummy began to growl. He was hungry! "It's a good thing I packed five loaves and two fish for my lunch today," the boy said to himself.

As the boy opened his lunch basket, he saw that the other men and their wives and children did not have any lunch. Then he heard Jesus ask, "Where do you think we can get enough bread to feed everyone in the crowd?"

The boy brought his lunch to Jesus' followers. "This isn't nearly enough food for everyone," said Andrew.

But Jesus made that little bit of lunch into more and more food. Soon everyone in the crowd—more than 5,000 men—had their fill of bread and fish. There were even leftovers.

The little boy was glad to share. Jesus made enough lunch for everyone there.

- What did the boy bring to eat for lunch?
- What is your favorite lunch to share?

Show & Tell

Now it's your child's turn. Say the rhyme together and help him show and tell that
- the boy shared five loaves and two fish.
- Jesus made enough food for more than 5,000 people to eat their fill.

Show the fork that brings food for your tummy.

Tell how a boy brought a lunch that was yummy.

Little loaves and small fish were the young boy's treat

but Jesus made it grow so the whole crowd could eat.

Jesus the Good Shepherd

I am the good shepherd; I know my sheep and my sheep know me. *John 10:14*

Give your fluffy little lamb a hug and a cuddle. Sheep are soft and cute, but they need a shepherd to take care of them and keep them safe. Jesus is like a good shepherd and we are like his sheep.

Jesus came to Earth to show people how much he cares for them. To help his followers understand this, he told stories about shepherds and sheep.

Jesus told a story of a shepherd who had a hundred sheep. When the shepherd lost one sheep, he left the ninety-nine to look for the one that was lost. When the shepherd found the lost sheep, he was so happy!

Jesus told a story of a good shepherd who called his sheep by their names. The sheep listened to his voice. The sheep followed the good shepherd. They were safe with him.

Jesus said, "I am the good shepherd. The good shepherd gives up his life to save the lives of his sheep."

The shepherd's voice is what his flock hears. The sheep stay safe when the shepherd is near.

- Pretend to *baa* like a little lost sheep.

- Who is like a good shepherd?

Show & Tell

Now it's your child's turn. Say the rhyme together and help her show and tell that

- Jesus is the good shepherd and we are his sheep.
- Jesus cares for us.

Show a fluffy lamb with wool to share.

Tell about the people in Jesus' care.

Jesus is our good shepherd guide.

We hear his voice and stay safe by his side.

Jesus' Healing Hands

"Lord," he said, "if you are willing, you can heal me and make me clean." *Luke 5:12*

Your hands can hold a crayon or give "high five" to a friend. You protect them from the cold winters by wearing warm gloves. Jesus' hands were a lot like yours. He used his hands to tie the strap of his sandals or pound a carpenter's hammer. There was another special thing Jesus' hands could do.

Jesus showed God's love for people. He showed God's care for sick people by making them well. He made blind people see. He made others able to walk. Many people heard about Jesus' healing power. They came to meet Jesus.

"Lord, if you want to, you could heal me," a poor, sick man said to Jesus one day. This man had a disease called leprosy. The man also had faith in Jesus' power to make him better.

Jesus reached out his hand and touched the man. "Be healed!" Jesus said. In an instant, the man's leprosy disappeared. The sores that had been on the man's skin were gone.

After that, even more sick people came to hear Jesus preach and ask him for help. The word quickly spread across the land that Jesus could heal with just a touch of his hand.

- What did Jesus do for people who were sick?
- What did Jesus do to heal the man with leprosy?

Show & Tell

Now it's your child's turn. Say the rhyme together and help him show and tell that
- Jesus showed God's love for people by healing them.
- Jesus touched a man with leprosy and made him well.

Show the gloves, warm and soft on your hand.
Tell of the hands that cared for a sick man.

The man said to Jesus, "Lord, heal me, please."

Jesus' touch cured the sick man's disease.

Zacchaeus' Money

"Zacchaeus!" he said. "Quick, come down! I must be a guest in your home today." Luke 19:5

You saved up coins in your piggy bank. Hear them rattle and clank as you give it a shake! Zacchaeus had jars full of coins as well. But some of that money was not really his. He cheated people to get it!

The coins in his pockets *jingle-jangled* together as Zacchaeus climbed the sycamore tree. He was not tall enough to see over the crowds, but if he climbed high enough, Zacchaeus was sure he could catch a glimpse of Jesus.

Jesus entered the town and soon he came to the foot of Zacchaeus' tree. He looked up and said, "Zacchaeus, come down! I am going to your house."

Zacchaeus had made a lot of money by collecting taxes. That's why the crowd was surprised when Jesus went to Zacchaeus' house. But Zacchaeus wanted to change his greedy ways. He was so glad to meet Jesus. He wanted to follow Jesus and start doing right. He told Jesus, "Now I will give to the poor and if I cheated, I will repay what I stole."

- Where did Jesus see Zacchaeus?
- Who gave you the money to save in your piggy bank?

Show & Tell

Now it's your child's turn. Say the rhyme together and help her show and tell that

- Jesus went to Zacchaeus' house.
- Zacchaeus gave to the poor and repaid what he had stolen.

Show your piggy with coins inside.
Tell of the man whom Jesus spied.

Zacchaeus loved money, but now loves Jesus more.

He returned what he stole and he gave to the poor.

Clinking Coins

She, poor as she is, has given everything she had.
Mark 12:43

What are some things you can buy with your coins? A new toy or a piece of candy? A gift for your mom? Jesus saw a poor woman with some coins in the temple one day. What did she do with her coins?

link, clink, clang! Pile after pile of coins landed in the chests in the courtyard. The gold, silver, and brass coins were offerings to God. The loud clatter of the money made everyone in the crowd know just how much some wealthy people were giving.

Jesus and his disciples were in the courtyard teaching about God. They heard the clinking coins landing in the collection chests. Then one woman came to give her offering. Two copper coins—worth less than one penny—dropped in. She gave such a small amount. What would Jesus say about this?

Jesus told his followers, "This woman is a widow. Those two coins were all the money she had. Even though her gift was a small amount, it has more value than the others."

The piles of coins made a loud clatter, but the size of a gift is not all that matters.

- What sound did the coins make as they dropped into the chest?
- How much money did the poor widow give?

Show & Tell

Now it's your child's turn. Say the rhyme together and help him show and tell that
- the poor widow gave two small coins.
- Jesus valued her gift more than the others.

Show the coins that you have saved.
Tell of the coins a poor woman gave.

Two copper pieces were all she possessed.

Jesus said she gave more than the rest.

Welcome with Palm Branches

A large crowd . . . took palm branches and went down
the road to meet him. *John 12:12, 13*

When your grandparents or your friends come to visit
your house, you welcome them and say, "I'm happy to see
you!" When Jesus entered the city of Jerusalem, the people
there were glad he came. They brought palm branches to
welcome him in a very special way.

The people of Jerusalem were happy to see Jesus coming. They had heard his wonderful teaching. They had seen him do amazing things. A large crowd of people gathered in the city.

The long leaves of the palm branches rustled as they brushed together. The people waved the branches at Jesus and dropped them onto the road. The palm branches were a way of giving Jesus honor. Step by step, the donkey colt carrying Jesus walked over the branches.

More and more people gathered around Jesus. They sang and shouted praises to him. They called Jesus their king. They said, "Praise God! Blessed is the one who comes in God's name!"

- How did the people show Jesus honor?

- What animal did Jesus ride on?

Show & Tell

Now it's your child's turn. Say the rhyme together and help her show and tell that
- Jesus entered Jerusalem riding on a donkey.
- the people honored and praised Jesus.

Show and wave the leafy branch that you found.
Tell of palm branches that were laid on the ground.

With palms for his path and praises for his ears

the people honored Jesus with shouts and cheers!

The Lord's Supper

"Do this to remember me." *Luke 22:19*

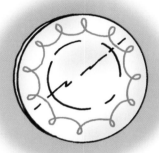

A meal is a time to fill your plate—and then your tummy—full of delicious food. A meal shared with your family is a time to talk and laugh together. How can remembering be a reason for a meal?

Jesus and his followers were eating a special meal, called Passover, together. Jesus and his friends passed the plates of vegetables and bread around the large table.

Soon Jesus would leave his followers. He knew that this was the last meal he would share with his friends. Jesus showed his followers a special way to always remember him. Jesus took some bread and gave thanks to God. Then he broke the bread, and passed it to his followers. He said, "Take and eat this bread."

Jesus took his cup and thanked God for it. He passed his cup to them too. He said, "Take and drink. Remember me when you eat this bread and drink from this cup."

When we eat and drink we remember Jesus and the things he did because he loves us.

- Can you imagine sharing a meal with Jesus sitting at your table?

- When did Jesus say we should remember him?

Show & Tell

Now it's your child's turn. Say the rhyme together and help him show and tell that

- Jesus ate a Passover meal with his followers.
- Jesus showed his followers a way to remember him when they eat and drink.

Show the plate that food fills to the rim.

Tell of the last meal Jesus' friends ate with him.

Jesus asked his followers to remember

whenever we drink and eat bread together.

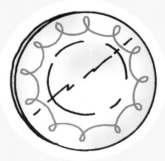

Jesus Died yet Lives Again

Jesus died and was raised to life again. *1 Thessalonians 4:14*

The cross you have is simple and beautiful. But in Jesus' time it was a terrible thing. Why would Jesus' followers choose a cross as a sign for their faith?

Jesus died on a cross on a terrible, dark day. This was the hard, sad thing that Jesus had to do to complete God's plan for saving people from sin.

His followers buried Jesus' body in a tomb and closed it with a heavy stone.

But when some women went back to Jesus' tomb, they were surprised to find the stone was rolled away and the tomb was empty! An angel appeared. "Jesus is not here," the angel told the women. "He rose to life again!"

Many people saw Jesus after he had risen. He told them, "Go everywhere and tell everyone the Good News about me!" Then he returned to Heaven.

Jesus died and lives again. He took our punishment for sin.

- Who did God send to save people from sin?
- What happened after Jesus died?

Show & Tell

Now it's your child's turn. Say the rhyme together and help her show and tell that
- Jesus died on a cross.
- Jesus came back to life again and now lives in Heaven.

Show your cross, the symbol Christians give.

Tell how Jesus died and yet lives.

A cross was the terrible yet wonderful place

where punishment for sin was met with God's grace.

The Way to Get Clean

Repent of your sins and turn to God, and be baptized in the name of Jesus Christ. *Acts 2:38*

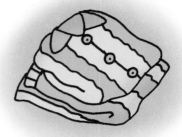

Pajamas are best when they are still warm from a tumble in the dryer. Soft and clean, they smell so fresh and make your nighttime comfy. A washing machine and dryer are the way to make pajamas clean. How can a person make his life clean?

After Jesus returned to Heaven, Peter and Jesus' other followers started doing the job Jesus had given them, which was to go everywhere and tell everyone the Good News about Jesus.

Peter preached, "We have all done wrong things. Doing wrong—sin—makes a big mess in our lives. God sent Jesus to make us clean again."

There were many people in the crowd listening to the message. Jesus' followers told them about all the wonderful things Jesus had done. They preached that Jesus had died and rose again. The people listened. They wanted to make their messy lives clean. They asked, "What should we do?"

Peter replied, "Repent and be baptized. Count on Jesus to clean up the mess that sin makes in your life." The people began to believe in Jesus. They repented—that means they turned away from sin. They were baptized that day and became a part of the new church.

- What was the job Jesus gave to his followers?
- What did Peter tell the people to do?

Show & Tell

Now it's your child's turn. Say the rhyme together and help him show and tell that

- sin in a person's life makes a mess that needs to be cleaned.
- Peter said, "Repent and be baptized."

Show your clean PJs, tidy and bright.

Tell of the way to get clean in God's sight.

Peter told the people that God washes away sin

then they turned to God and began life again.

Tabitha's Kindness

There was a believer in Joppa named Tabitha. . . . She was always doing kind things for others. *Acts 9:36*

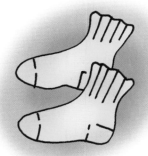

A winter's night by the fire can be so wonderful and cozy. Bundle up in your warmest socks and your fuzziest PJs! But imagine if winter were coming and you didn't have any warm clothes to wear. The Bible tells about some people who had that problem, but Tabitha knew just what to do about it.

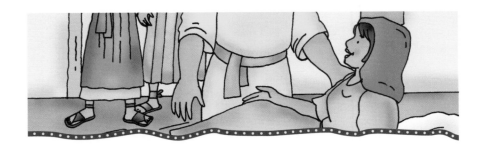

Tabitha was a busy woman. She worked very hard sewing clothes; a light, breezy shirt for summer, and a heavy, warm cloak for winter. Tabitha showed she loved Jesus by giving the clothes she made to people who were poor.

One day Tabitha became very ill and she died. Her friends and all the poor people she had helped were so sad. They sent a message to Jesus' disciple Peter. "Please come quickly!" they begged Peter.

As soon as Peter arrived, Tabitha's friends took him to the room where her body lay. They showed him all the beautiful clothes and coats she had made for them. God gave Peter special power. He was able to make Tabitha live again. "Get up!" Peter said to Tabitha. Then she opened her eyes and sat up! Everyone was so happy to have their friend back.

Tabitha came back to life once more. She could soon work again making clothes for the poor.

- Have you ever given to someone in need? How did it make you feel?
- What did Peter say to Tabitha?

Show & Tell

Now it's your child's turn. Say the rhyme together and help her show and tell that

- Tabitha made clothes to give to the poor.
- Peter raised Tabitha from the dead.

Show the socks that warm up your toes.

Tell of those who needed warm clothes.

Tabitha saw the poor and their needs.

She gave and so was loved for her deeds.

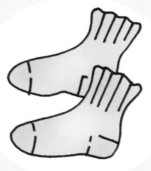

Paul's Beautiful Feet

How beautiful are the feet of messengers who bring good news! *Romans 10:15*

Wearing sandals gives you dusty feet and sun-tanned toes. The leather slaps pleasantly as you walk down the road. The sandals on Paul's feet pounded over miles and miles of dusty roads. Paul traveled on a mission.

Paul walked along the roads—from Jerusalem to Athens to Rome and back again. He traveled from city to city preaching the good news about Jesus. He said, "Have faith in Jesus and your sins will be forgiven."

Many people who heard Paul's words decided to follow Jesus. Wherever Paul went, churches began to grow. But in some towns, Paul's message made people angry. They accused Paul of stirring up trouble. Some people tried to kill Paul. Other times he was put in jail. Still Paul would not stop preaching and praising God.

Paul kept on walking from city to city. Paul preached, "You can live the right way with Jesus' help." Paul marched on until he could march no more. Then he wrote letters to the churches he had visited. Paul spread the good news.

Paul walked across the world with sandals on his feet. He talked about Jesus to each person he would meet.

- Why did Paul travel across the world?
- What did people do when they heard Paul's preaching about Jesus?

Show & Tell

Now it's your child's turn. Say the rhyme together and help him show and tell that
- Paul traveled all over the world.
- Paul preached about Jesus everywhere.

Show off the shoes that you wear down the street.

Tell of Paul's sandals and his busy feet.

God always showed Paul which roads to go down

as he carried God's message to each city and town.

Lydia Believes in Jesus

As she listened to us, the Lord opened her heart. *Acts 16:14*

Do you have a purple ball or a purple shirt? The purple thing you have gets its color from something called *dye*. Lydia had a job selling dye. Her job brought her wealth, but the good news she heard one day brought her something even better—a friendship with Jesus.

Lydia was a wealthy, important woman who had an important job. She earned money by selling purple dye—a very expensive and luxurious item. Her customers were rich rulers and kings.

Lydia was also a good and wise woman. She knew that the money she earned and the status she had were not the most important things. Lydia loved God and prayed to him. Lydia and some other women met together at the edge of the river to pray. One day while they were praying, they met some of Jesus' followers: Paul and Silas.

Paul began teaching the women the good news about Jesus' love for them. Lydia listened to Paul's message. She decided to follow Jesus too. So she was baptized along with all of the people in her household.

Lydia wanted to help Paul keep preaching in her town. She invited Paul and his helper, Silas, to stay at her house. She said, "I truly believe in Jesus, just like you do. Please come and be my guests."

- What was Lydia's important job?
- What was Lydia doing when she met Paul?

Show & Tell

Now it's your child's turn. Say the rhyme together and help her show and tell that
- Lydia was a seller of purple dye.
- Lydia heard Paul's message about Jesus and became a Christian.

Show your purple cloth—a blend of red and blue.
Tell of the people Lydia sold purple to.

She heard Paul's message by the riverside.

She believed and with her family was baptized.

Many Pieces in One Whole

We are many parts of one body, and we all belong to each other. *Romans 12:5*

A puzzle is one large picture made up of many smaller pieces. Some of the pieces have different colors. Some pieces make up the edge of the picture. Some are in the middle. Just as each piece has its job to do in making up the puzzle-picture, so each person has a job to do in the church.

All over the world people had begun to believe in Jesus and become his followers. A group of believers praying and worshipping together was called the church.

The churches were made up of different kinds of people. Some were slaves. Some were rich. Some spoke a different language. Paul told the different people in the church, "Even though you have differences, you share the most important thing: You believe in Jesus."

The people in the church used their skills and talents to do work for Jesus. Not everyone had the same skill. Some people were teachers and leaders. Other people were helpers.

Paul compared the church to a person's body. A body needs the feet to do the walking and the eyes to see. Paul said, "All of you must work together, doing different jobs. You are each a part of one body—Jesus' body."

- What do we call groups of Jesus' followers who pray and worship together?
- What different kinds of people can be part of a church?

Show & Tell

Now it's your child's turn. Say the rhyme together and help him show and tell that
- the church is one body with many parts.
- people have different jobs in the church.

Show the pieces of a puzzle that's fun.

Tell how many pieces combine to make one.

The church is like a body with eyes, hands, and feet.

People are the parts that make a church complete!

Greetings and Love

Greet each other with Christian love. *1 Corinthians 16:20*

It's fun to get mail! You tear open the envelope with your name on it to see the message inside. Have you ever gotten mail from God? When people first began following Jesus, they sometimes received important news, instructions, and encouragement in the mail.

Everywhere in the world, more and more churches were beginning to grow. Missionaries like Paul visited many of the churches to help them learn more about Jesus and how to be Jesus' followers.

Sometimes churches needed more instructions or help to understand. When that happened, God told Paul or another teacher the message he wanted the churches to hear. The teacher wrote letters and sent the important words to the people across the world.

We can read God's letters today. They make up a large part of the Bible. What kinds of things did these letters say?

One letter, the letter to the Romans says, "There is nothing anywhere that can separate us from God's love." The letter to the Corinthians says, "The greatest thing in the world is love. Loving is our highest goal."

- How did God give messages to the church?
- Where can we read God's letters?

Show & Tell

Now it's your child's turn. Say the rhyme together and help her show and tell that

- God's words were written in letters to the church.
- the Bible contains God's message to us.

Show the card that was sent to you.

Tell of the letter with words that are true.

Paul wrote down the message God gave.

His letters told churches how to live the right way.

The Fruit of the Spirit

Let the Holy Spirit guide your lives. *Galatians 5:16*

What do you get when you plant an apple tree in your yard? You get apples! What if you plant a pear tree? You get pears, of course. How can the Holy Spirit cause a person to bear fruit?

The Bible says you can tell what kind of tree you have by looking at the fruit it gives. The choices we make—either good or bad—are like fruit growing on the trees of our lives. Sometimes it's hard to get along with your sister. Sometimes you wait for your little brother to catch up or help your dad clean. If you fight with your sister, is that bearing good or bad fruit?

The Holy Spirit is the helper Jesus sends to his followers so we can make the best choices and bear good fruit. The Holy Spirit helps us show love. He fills us with joy, peace, and patience. He helps us be kind, good, and faithful. He teaches us to be gentle and to have self-control. These good things are the fruit of the Spirit.

Having the Holy Spirit is one of the best things about being a follower of Jesus. Guided by the Holy Spirit, a Christian girl or boy can have a life that's filled with love, patience, peace, and joy.

- How can you tell an apple tree from a pear tree?

- What helper does Jesus send to his followers?

Show & Tell

Now it's your child's turn. Say the rhyme together and help him show and tell that
- the Holy Spirit is the helper Jesus sends to his followers.
- one fruit of the Spirit is love.

Show the fruit that is a treat to eat.

Tell of fruit that makes a Christian's life sweet.

Love, joy, and peace fill the thoughts and deeds

of a Christian who follows the Holy Spirit's lead.

Put on the Armor of God

Put on all of God's armor so that you will be able to
stand firm. *Ephesians 6:11*

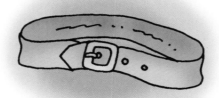

Take your belt and cinch it up tight. Its job is to hold up
your pants and look stylish. The Bible tells about a belt that
has a different kind of job. It is a part of the armor that
helps you win a fight!

S̲tomp, stomp, stomp. A line of Roman soldiers marched past Jesus' follower, Paul. The soldiers were wearing their heavy armor—ready to fight any enemy that might come. Paul wrote about the soldiers and their armor in a lesson for Christians about the fight against our enemy, Satan.

Satan is an enemy who wants to see Jesus' followers fail to love God and do right things. We must fight against him, but not with armor made of metal. Paul wrote, "Put on God's armor. It will protect you against Satan's tricks!

"Buckle truth around your waist like a belt. Wear God's righteousness like a breastplate. For shoes, put on the peace that comes from the Good News that Jesus saves us from sin. Hold up a shield of faith. Put on salvation as your helmet. God's Word, the Bible, is like a sword."

Keep praying for God to help you win the battle. With this armor, God gives strength to fight against Satan and his nasty tricks.

- Who is a tricky enemy?

- What are some of the pieces of God's armor?

Show & Tell

Now it's your child's turn. Say the rhyme together and help her show and tell that

- Satan is an enemy who wants Christians to fail.
- God's armor protects us against Satan's attacks.

Show the belt worn in your waistband.
Tell of the armor that helps you to stand.

God's armor makes you strong in his might

so you'll be ready for a spiritual fight.

Timothy Learns and Studies

Be an example to all believers in what you say, in the way you live, in your love, your faith, and your purity.
1 Timothy 4:12

Learning something new can be hard work. But toys that teach the ABCs and 123s can make it fun. The Bible tells us Timothy learned and studied too. He learned about faith in Jesus and he studied God's Word.

Lois had a daughter named Eunice. Eunice had a son named Timothy. When Lois learned about Jesus and his salvation, she taught the good news to Eunice. Then she and Eunice together taught the good news to Timothy.

Timothy followed the good teaching of his mother and grandmother. He loved and studied God's Word. Timothy became a missionary and joined Paul on his journeys. He traveled to many places, preaching about Jesus. Timothy loved and cared for the people at the places he visited.

The apostle Paul wrote to Timothy, "Learn to be like Jesus. Keep teaching people to live the way God wants. Be an example to Jesus' followers in what you say and do."

- Who taught Timothy about faith in Jesus?
- What did Timothy study?

Show & Tell

Now it's your child's turn. Say the rhyme together and help him show and tell that
- Timothy studied God's Word.
- Timothy preached about Jesus and set an example.

Show the toy with letters ABC.

Tell of the lessons taught to Timothy.

God's truth was what Timothy learned and then

   preached

and he set an example in faith, life, and speech.

A Colorful City

Look, God's home is now among his people! He will live
with them, and they will be his people. *Revelation 21:3*

Imagine a perfect, beautiful new home. It has rooms for
everyone you love. It is filled with beautiful things. Nothing
sad could ever happen there. Can you draw a picture of it
with your crayons? Be sure to use plenty of colors and add
Jesus to your picture too. The perfect new home is what
Jesus is making for his followers—in Heaven.

Jesus had told his followers, "I will make a new home for you in Heaven. One day I will bring you all there and we can be together." His followers did not know what Heaven would be like. They only knew it must be a wonderful place because Jesus was there. Then one day, Jesus showed a picture of Heaven to his follower, John.

The place was like a new city, more beautiful than anything John had ever seen before. It was made of blue sapphire and purple amethyst. John described green and red gems and precious metals. John wrote, "God's glory lights up the whole city and it sparkles like a diamond. The streets are made out of pure gold. The city gates are made of shimmery pearls."

The people who love Jesus get to be at home with him. There is no sadness or tears or pain. The bad is gone and everything has been made new.

- What is the name of the wonderful new home Jesus is

  making for his followers?

- What colors did John use to describe the new city?

206

Show & Tell

Now it's your child's turn. Say the rhyme together and help her show and tell that

- Heaven is like a beautiful new city.
- one day all of Jesus' followers will be together with Jesus in Heaven.

Show your crayons—red, green, and blue.

Tell of a holy city made new.

John's vision of Heaven shimmers and shines

with brilliant jewel colors only God could design.